The Role of Spiritual Caregivers to the Terminally Ill Patients

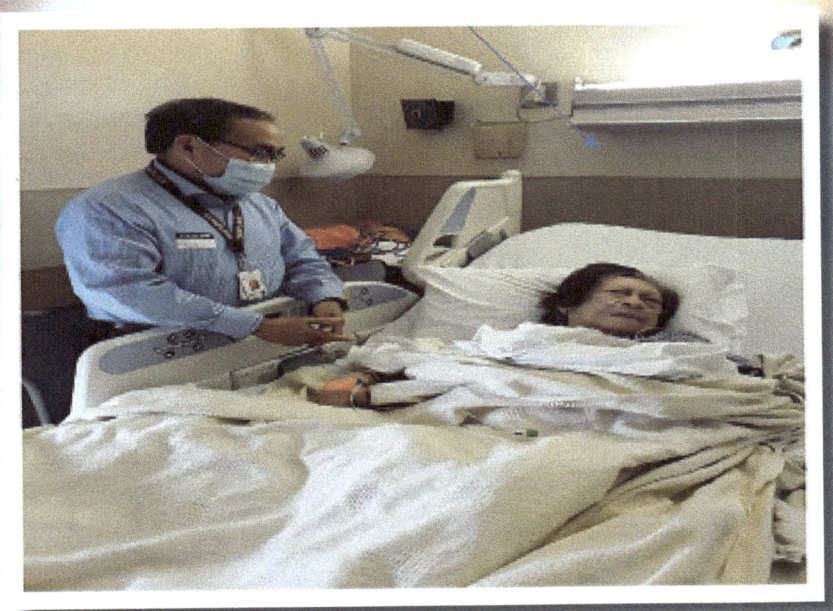

A Resource Manual

Jim Garcines

The Role of Spiritual Caregivers to the Terminally Ill Patients

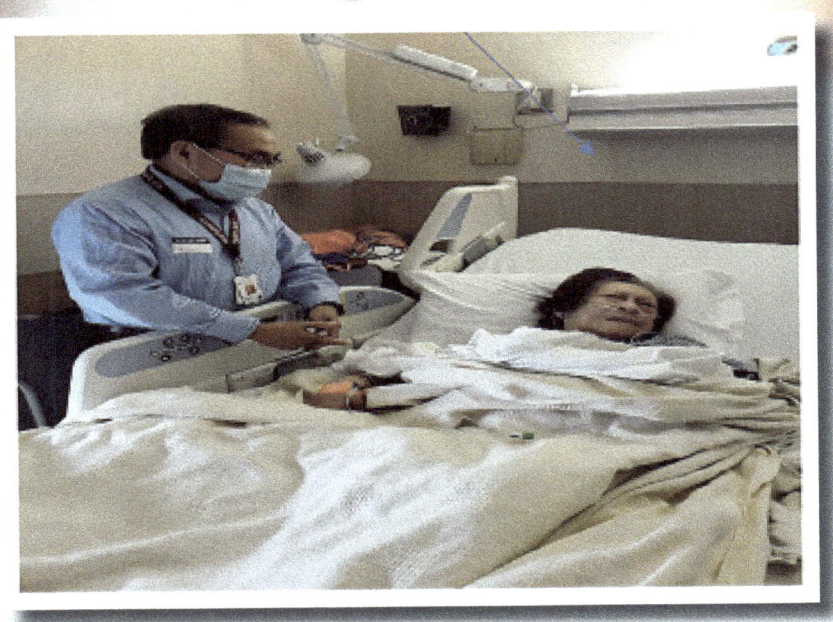

A Resource Manual

Jim Jareines

ARPress

ARPress
45 Dan Road Suite 5
Canton MA 02021

Hotline·   1(888) 821-0229
Fax·   1(508) 545-7580

Ordering Information·

Quantity sales. Special discounts are available on quantity purchases by corporations, associations, and others. For details, contact the publisher at the address above.

Printed in the United States of America.

ISBN-13·   Paperback   979-8-89356-230-9
              eBook   979-8-89356-231-6

Library of Congress Control Number· 2024908941

CONTENTS

DEDICATION

To my dearest wife, Carol, who taught, encouraged and inspired my tough journey with God. She was a great help as I write this manual. She is a godly woman, a mentor whose life immensely touch's lives as she teaches children, parents and women in our church. But above all, she raised our two children in the path of God. To my daughter, Jica who's unending support to complete the draft. To my son, Jeriah who's determination to explore my Spiritual intervention more of this draft. My daughter in law- Lheianne for praying and my grand daughter Solenn who give me constant smile and music through "the laughter of this innocent child." I'm blessed to have my family a very good support in this endeavor!

I. Introduction

I am privileged and have great opportunity to work in the hospital, where I had been exposed to and experience several needs in pastoral care. I had visited countless patients each day as I do my rounds to various departments in varied situations and conditions as well as responding to Code Blue. My daily experience had taught me a lot on how to effectively minister to patients who are terminally ill and dying. Several times, I feel hurt and sympathetic other than the family of patients. I am the first one absorbing all the agonies, regrets, failures, misery, anger, hurts of the patients as they share what they are going through in their conditions which taught me to be more humble, compassionate and prayerful person. I've seen over three decades of my pastoral ministry with different congregations this ministry has enhance my role as a caregiver. Let me share with you my personal experience with my sister who got stroke few years ago and become diabetic that her health conditions had no shown any progress but instead had deteriorate and getting serious that has affected me most since I am the one who is always in constant contact with her and shown more care about her situation. The Doctor told me that her condition is getting worst and deteriorating each day, I thought of ministering to her most often while she still in a Nursing home until her two feet is amputated and become more helpless and hopeless and become terminally ill. Because of this experience this has given me an insight of what I can do and be of help to those who are in the same boat as I do to a terminally ill and dying patient. May this Resource Manual will offer support for those who are engage in pastoral care.

The following lines is my heartfelt suggestions to all pastoral caregivers, that they can be equipped in ministering to patients as they engage to helping them in their needs especially those who are in palliative and hospice conditions. Please note that the word "*Palliative and Hospice*" have strong connotations.

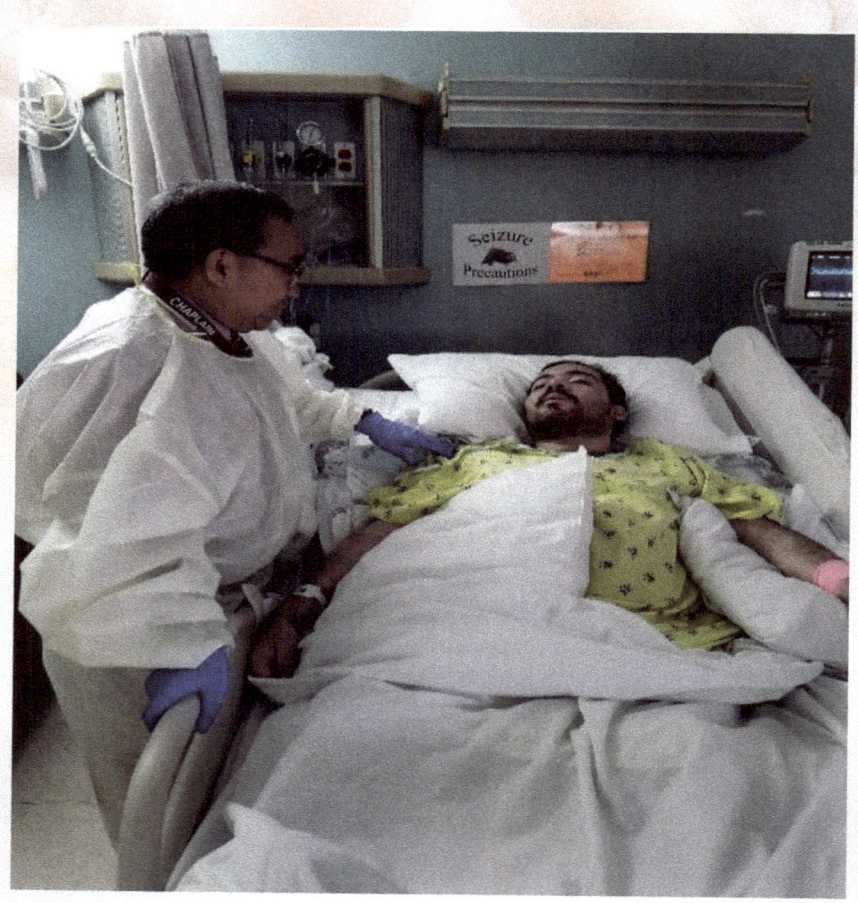

Palliative Care can be defined as an approach that improves the quality of life of patients and families facing life-threatening illness through the prevention, assessment and treatment of physical, psycho-social or spiritual suffering. Palliative Care can be delivered along with life-prolonging treatments or as the main focus of care. Palliative Care is for all patients with chronic or life-limiting conditions regardless of life expectancy.

Hospice is a specific type of palliative care that is actually the most intense form of palliative care. Hospice is considered when patients have less than 6 months to life. Patients agree to enroll in hospice program and choose not to receive aggressive care.(3) Janice Noort, NP wrote that "Effective and sensitive spiritual care is extremely important for those whom death is imminent. Spiritual needs are very complicated and often difficult to discuss since spirituality and religion are sensitive and personal topics. The role of the spiritual caregiver in palliative care is to be open, listen, observe and when in doubt, ask questions. Performing a spiritual assessment and evaluating for spiritual distress are important aspects of the role of the spiritual caregiver for the dying patient. Essential skills necessary include deep listening and providing a peaceful presence which require human kindness, compassion and caring."3

Ministry to the terminally ill and dying patients, as well as with the families is one of the most sacred privileges of the pastor. It is the time when many people want their pastors to be near them.

Our effectiveness in the ministry will be based on how well we have integrated into life what is believed about death and about life.

A hospital chaplain once said, "We have learned that unless pastors are at peace with their mortality and its vast implications, they are not free to accompany others in dying. Fulfillment in death can come only when one's life perspective adequately answers the question of meaning and purpose in the realm of destiny."9 Basic to the Christian ministry is a life perspective which offers such interpretation. The revelation of Jesus Christ discloses the reality of God's love for us and reveals his concern for man's destiny.

Denial is a natural emotional response. It protects the ego and is necessary if the person is to distinguish between inevitability of death and the imminence of death. Family and friends are torn between being forced by circumstances to surrender the dying person and being forced by the emotional ties of love to hold on to the patient as long as possible. Love ones often tell dying persons how much they are needed, the life they can't go on without them, and they encourage them to fight to the very end. As pastoral caregivers, we face a lot of questions that needs answers as we minister to these kinds of patients. Here are some ideas that we need to consider:

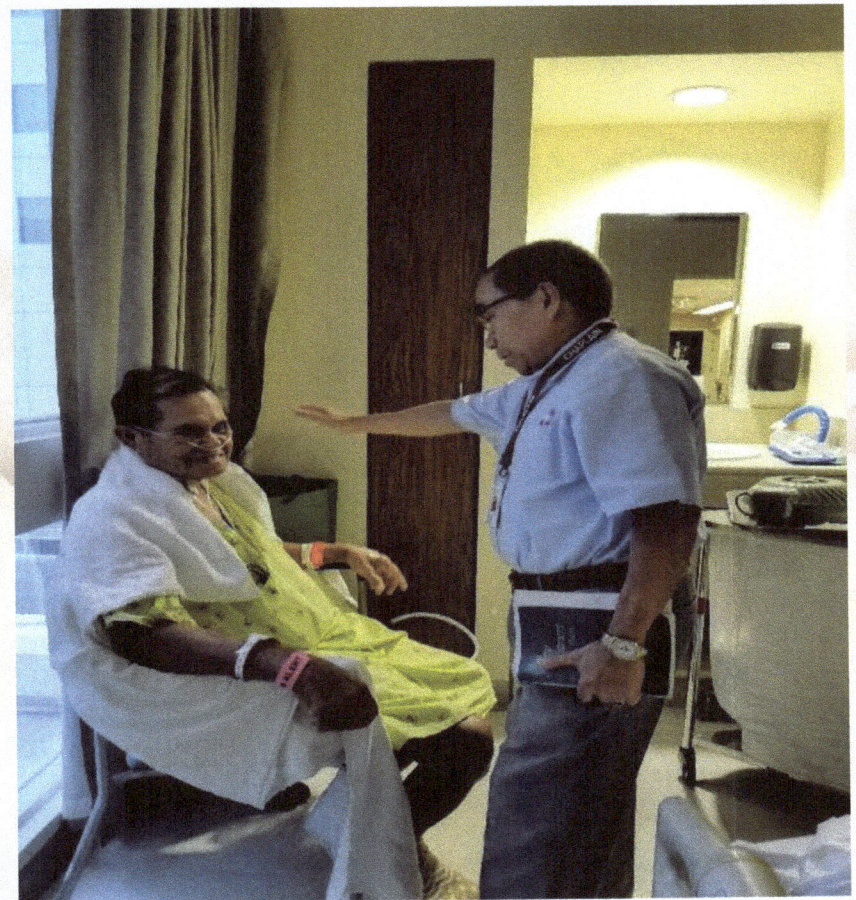

II. The Requisite of the Spiritual Caregivers

A. Preparation Spiritual Caregivers

Pastor's enactment of his role with hospitalized parishioners plays an important part during the crisis of illness. He must learn to understand patient and physician relationships, coping with illness in the family as well as family concerns during illness. Providing basic support is essential, just being there and caring while at the same time symbolically representing the love of God.

The sharing of the scripture and prayer as well as counseling can refocus values, assist decision making, affirms relationship is very important. Pastor's preparation must also be on going by participating in Clinical Pastoral Education program. If C.P.E. is unavailable, there are other ways to grow as helping person during life crises. A senior minister who is willing to be mentor can be an alternative.

B. Provision of Ministerial Caregivers

It is not uncommon for ministers to be impressed to the point of intimidation at how concrete and measurable are the tasks performed by most health professionals. In an effort to compensate, I have seen pastors become activists in hospital visitation, expressing anxiety through attempts at humor, taking dirty laundry home to be washed, or going to gift shop to buy newspaper. This suggests a lack of clarity in pastoral identity, heightened somewhat by the loss of status and skilled task performed by others. Few people enter the patient's room with the task of listening to them. Yet, feelings and concerns, values, self-image, and faith issues are storm inside, needing to be shared. This is the strength of the pastoral role—to be able to sit and listen with understanding. The patient needs to feel blessed by feeling enough worth that someone would be concerned to hear what the illness experience is like. Self-worth that is normally defined by doing or productivity is unavailable to the patient. Discovering worth is simply being elusive, until you have the experience of being listened to with attendant emotions of being accepted and forgiven.

Our ministry to the terminally ill is to be a listener. Simple reflection, a touch and a listening ear will minister and speak volumes. This skill of listening is hard work, because when done well, the ear is informed by good counseling skills, relevant knowledge, and the wisdom of faith. It is most active process. The minister cannot count incisions stitches, or medicines prescribed to measure worth. Being clear about the pastoral role is crucial to the enactment of it, particularly during crisis experiences. I asked some questions to medical persons at UC Davis Medical Center, Sacramento, CA and found answers that are beneficial to our care. Here are their insights and understanding regarding terminally ill patients as well as people around them.

1. *What are the emotional reactions you see when you tell patients their diagnosis of terminal illness?*

• My experience is that patient and family typically display the various stages of grief— denial, anger, bargaining, depression, and acceptance in addition to anxiety. The stages they go through are not experienced in any particular order. Occasionally patients and/or family remain "stuck" in one stage such as anger or depression and sometimes the stage of acceptance is never attained!(3)

• As one could imagine, the reactions of patients are quite varied. Many patients have suspected that they are quite ill and have a very bad illness and are not very surprised by the information. Many other patients, especially patients with young/teenage children are quite despondent and their first response is to think about their children and their needs. Many of those patients become angry and immediately vow to "beat their illness". The third typical reaction is patient is shocked by the news and basically shuts down emotionally and is unable to engage in any more meaningful conversation at that time. The most important thing for me to remember is to make sure I have time to be able to deliver the information and be as present for the patient and family as I can be. I never appear rushed. I am prepared to just listen and answer questions. I do not try and deliver too much information as they are usually not in a frame of mind to remember much. (4)

• I see full spectrum of reactions from denial to anger to acute distress/sadness. (1)

2. *How do you prepare the family for the final end of loved ones?*

• I feel it is important the family receive necessary education regarding the dying process and also have the emotional/spiritual support they need during this difficult time. People have many different ideas about the dying process and for many it is their first experience in dealing with death. It is essential that families receive information on what to expect so the mystery associated with death is removed and they understand death is a natural, inevitable process. I encourage questions and make every attempt to provide needed information in a way that is able to be understood. There are times family members do not want to discuss dying at length and I am respectful of their wishes. I will have the chaplains and social workers get involved for additional support when appropriate. (3)

- The simplest questions to help families is to ask them, "What are you most concerned about for your loved one?", "What are you or your loved one most worried about", "What information or questions answered do you need to help you through this process", "How is it that I can best help you and your loved one". (4)

- I try to be frank in my discussion of their loved one's terminal illness. I do not want to give them false hope. I need them to be as best prepared as they can be to handle the upcoming issues. I offer as much emotional support as I can and be sure we fully optimize support for home once patient discharged. (1)

3. *How do you cope with the stress in dealing with terminally ill?*

- Palliative care team members are definitely at high risk of developing compassion fatigue due to the associated stress. I find working in a multidisciplinary team with a shared goal helps me cope. Through collaboration and communication, we can be more effective which helps control stress. As a palliative care team, we also try to focus on team building activities to create a support system for one other. I have found it is also important to develop a sense of self awareness and practice self-care activities, including exercise, relaxation, socialization with friends/family and reading. I try to acknowledge my limitations and ask for help when I need it. I attempt to maintain a sense of balance in my life and think it's important to keep one's sense of humor! (3)

• It is emotionally taxing to deal with the terminal patient and their families. I feel personal sadness for patients and their families. It is important to recognize your own emotion and the vulnerability that you feel in working with such patients. Self care is the most important thing to help. Taking time for your personal needs whatever they are is important to recharge yourself. It is also important to realize that one can not fix everything and we should not feel that it is our job to do so, but rather many times it is just important to be present with patient and family, acknowledge the stress, emotion, etc but not try and fix it. (4)

• I have learned to separate my work from my personal life. Leave the stresses/emotions at work, for work. (1)

4. *How do you handle hostility from family members?*

• I try to remember that the goal is not to prevent a family member from experiencing emotions such as anger, sadness, fear, and loss since these are normal responses. I feel my role is to maintain a trusting therapeutic relationship and safe/supportive environment that allows emotions to be expressed in a positive way if possible. I try to legitimize the appropriateness/ normalcy of their reaction and try to explore what is underneath the emotion. I believe it is important to show empathy and explore strengths/copies strategies if possible. I often involve

C. Prayer Partner, Scripture and Sacraments

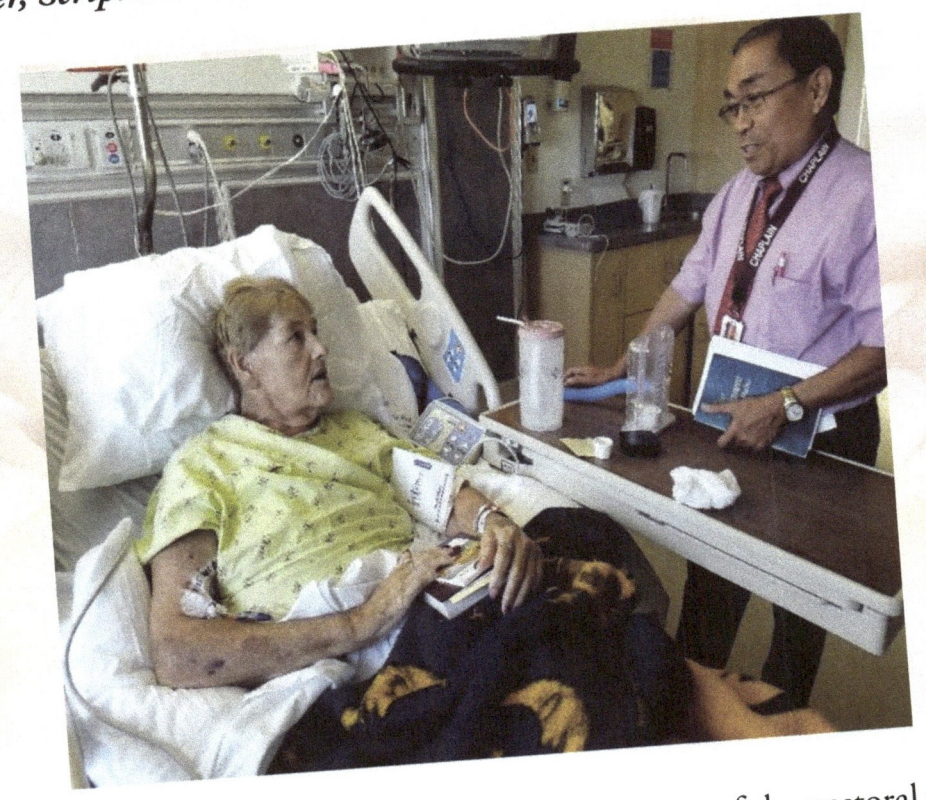

Most clergy agree that prayer is necessary and appropriate part of the pastoral visit. Let us begin with a basic theological foundation of prayer. We affirm first that God is present with us always seeking healing for us; God doesn't send illness for punishment. Even though all of us know this, it is easy for a person who is ill to revert to superstitious religion which suggests that this is particular affliction maybe willed by God. We participate in a world of nature set free which has all kinds of capacity to become destructive. But God does not equal nature. John A. T. Robinson says "that God does not cause the cancer, but God's face may be found in the cancer." This means that God is ever present, always with us, always accessible, always struggling in us and

Beyond the sharing of prayers and scriptures, the sacraments offer opportunities for healing mediated through the elemental symbols of the faith. The sacraments link the patient with God and the community of faith. Yet it often feels cumbersome to administer the sacrament in the hospital room. Some patients feel that the communion is a suggestion of terminal illness, so it is important to determine the patient's wishes and discuss the spirit in which the sacrament is offered. If the patient does wish to share communion, make sure there is no medical problem in his receiving the elements. Then find out if this is something he wishes to share with the family or friends or if he prefers to receive it alone.

If the room is shared with another patient, ask the neighboring patient if he wishes to share the sacrament. Explain your understanding of the openness of the sacrament and respect that patient's preference. Notify the nurse's station what you will be doing and ask that you be not disturbed during the period of time. Another thing if patient do not indicate belief in God, you can use nature to relate himself, or write some papers about their beliefs or use poems or traditions that they practice. Have them relate it and listen to what they say about their faith and way of life.

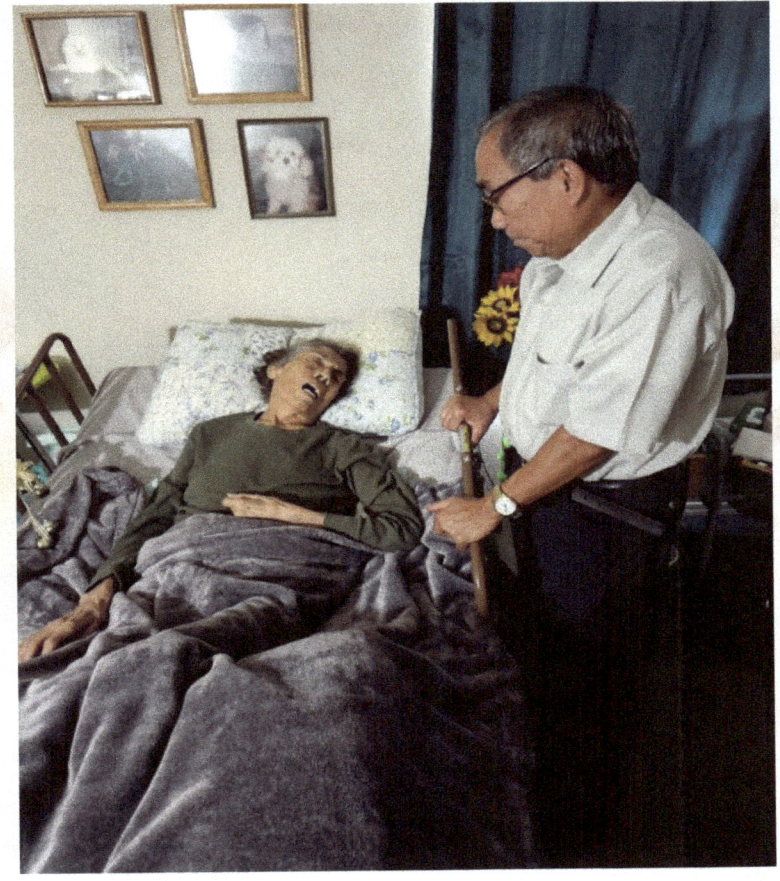

III. The Responsibility of the Spiritual Caregivers

A. Perspective on Period of time

There is a great challenge for us to be involved in the ministry especially to the terminally ill or dying patient. The responsibility to be a good minister depends on us. Many illnesses which will shorten life are chronic in nature and extend over a period of several years. This means that much important work must be done prior to death Bereavement or grief work is a process of adjustment which both acute and chronic phases, often lasting several years or longer beyond the patient's death. Pastoral Care begins at the point of diagnosis and is not completed until a reasonable adjustment to the loss has been achieved, usually several years later. The notion of fulfilling the pastoral role through the funeral rituals is superficial, at best.

B. Plans for living through serious illness

Living with and through serious illness is like running an ultra-marathon. It requires thoughtful planning, patience, endurance and timely support. Although, no one wants to experience it, this type of crisis has the potential of enriching relationships and of being a way into a more meaningful life. It is enough that the potential for goodness resides in what we would all agree is a life event no one would choose to experience. The patient suffering from a terminal illness may experience many behaviors and feelings which are generally useful for helpers to understand. These feelings include shock, fear, numbness, guilt, anger depression, lethargy, sadness, self-indulgence, and a host of others. They are normal but not comfortable feeling. Behaviors usually range between the polarities of accepting or denying the realities of illness. This is normal and the minister should be prepared for wide variations in the patients' or families focus on reality. Dying person may want to discuss funeral plans, and sometimes the pastor is the only one willing to talk about the approaching death. Planning for the funeral, need not be morbid, or maybe a means of accepting the reality of death, both the dying person and the family. Patient may want to receive communion as death draws near, make a public profession of faith and be baptized, or reaffirm his or her faith in preparation for death. If this form of rituals is acceptable with the patient, you may do so administer with love.

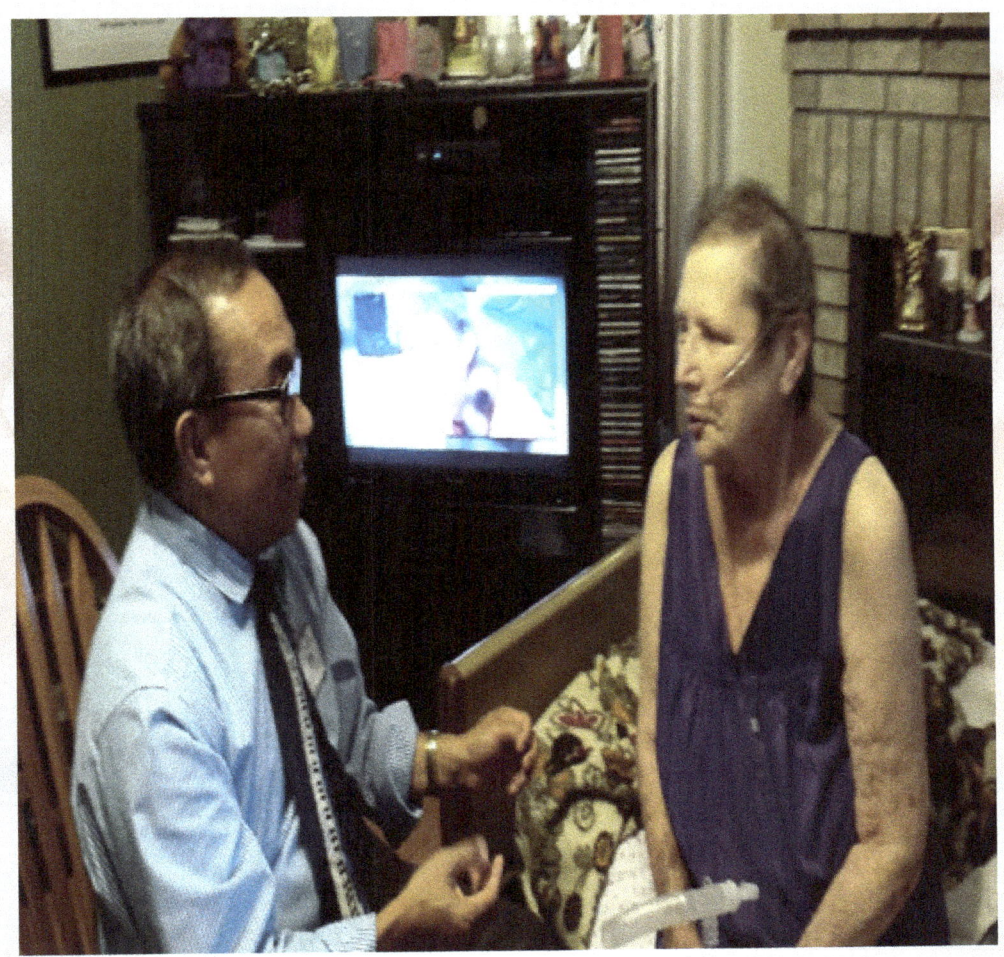

C. Painful Events

Few persons are prepared to live with serious illness or face losing a cherished loved one. Our culture highlights youth, vitality, and health. It cloisters painful events. Most people receive medical treatment and die away from home. As a result, even though everyone experiences death, preparation is rarely part of normal developmental experience. It is helpful, therefore, for patients and family to have guides, teachers, or counselors to facilitate their way through what amounts to a "foreign country." Health care professional will naturally have opportunities for intervention due to the role of the hospital. The largest time periods, however, will be those in the home community where the pastor is a primary resource.

D. Patients with Bioethical Issues

Another aspect of awareness for the Spiritual caregiver is the possibility of significant bio-ethical issues in decision-making. In the case of terminal illness, modern medicine has the ability to sustain life beyond what is meaningful existence. Decisions to withhold or withdraw life-sustaining treatment require careful thought. If the patient is comatose, it is usually the family which must decide. In some states "natural death" acts recognize express wishes of the patient in some form of the "Living Will" even he or she becomes comatose. But the specifics of the law must be observed, and they vary between states having such law. Theological and ethical positions must be considered by the pastor prior to being in a decision-making mode. They must include the ability to support families while minimizing feelings of guilt. The President's Commission has produced a series of publications regarding bioethical issues.

IV. The Resolutions of the Spiritual Caregivers

A. Prognosis and Diagnosis

When a patient had been told of the diagnosis and prognosis of his illness, he begun to struggle whether to live or die. It will prompt himself to take medication or adhere to therapy or undergo some surgery. Or will it depress or demoralize him that will lead to more rapid loss of health, or will it consider her suicide? Will telling them deprive them of happy days without worry or will it give them an opportunity to bring closer to their life? When they learn that they are so ill they go through stages described by Elizabeth Kubler-Ross which are: First, the stage of **denial**: the diagnosis wrong, the doctors are stupid. The second stage is **anger**: if only the doctor had run the correct test, I wouldn't be dying now. If only I had eaten vegetables, I wouldn't have cancer. The third stage is **bargaining**, the dying person may try to bargain for cure and recovery. The fourth stage is **realistic hope**, if recovery or cure is impossible the person may come to hope simply that the dying maybe prolonged or won't give much pain or expense to the family. The last stage is **acceptance**, the person may be able to affirm death as the natural fulfillment of life, the completion of its meaning as and purpose; though he may withdraw from those around him, on senses a spirit of peace equanimity.2 Families can accept death when the dying person has been able to find meaning. A dying person can conclude life with a sense of "It is finished" and let go, knowing that their pilgrimage was not in vain. As a pastor, you can approach them by being positive without expecting that you are going to cheer them up. Be prepared for their feeling of depression which can be an appropriate reaction to the thought of dying. Your job is to be a manifestation of God's love for and presence to them. When in doubt, try to imagine how Jesus would treat them and act accordingly. Pray for them.

B. Personal needs

1. *Physical*—Persons who are terminally ill experience worsening symptoms. For example, skin conditions, allergies, or spastic colon may worsen. More serious conditions such as ulcerative colitis, lupus, sarcoid, hypertension and asthma may flare up, due to stress in the immune system. Scripture reading is appropriate in line with the physical condition of the patient. Always close in prayer for healing, courage, power, strength and hope.

2. *Emotional*—Patients who are dying can be weepy and depressed, or angry. They can say hateful words, hurtful things while at the same time wanting to be understood. Some who are terminally ill of cancer or aids are not open and honest about their condition because of the societal stigma against person with this disease. They may be embarrassed of pastoral visit, thinking that they will be rejected. Some are even frightened because of the medical equipment hooked up to them. As a minister, do not act fearful because they might retreat emotionally from you. Do not look shocked because they might conclude that they are closer to the end of their lives than they really are. As a minister of God, you are a representative of God's love. If you make another visit do not be surprised if the vitality diminishes. The work of dying saps one's energy. So, he may be less willing to communicate than at other visits. Respect that, all you need to do is be present; God will do the rest. Pray with the patient if he wishes but do not insist on it. Allow him to voice his own prayer, if he wishes. Don't be surprised if the prayers are full of anger at whoever caused the illness or at God.

3. *Spiritual*—Spiritually people with terminal illness have serious questions about God's motives in permitting them to be so ill. Some even hate God so they don't want to pray, hear about God or see anyone from the church or pastor. Many question the existence of God or question the goodness of God why he permits them to suffer. Some patient wonders if God is punishing them for their past sins by giving them this sickness so they reject the overtures of pastoral visitors, who are after all, emissaries of the God whom they question. They may be angry at God and direct these feelings toward the pastoral visitors. Others, they may be

empty, unable to pray and unable to express their feelings about God. They may feel as if they are in a dessert or a wasteland. They may feel too disconsolate or too misunderstood to even hope for someone—especially a pastoral person—who can understand them. At the moment, this is the best time to share the Gospel to patients and reconcile them to God and experience the peace that they need as they come to the end of their journey. You need to prepare the soul of the patients for Eternity and assurance of God's love and care by putting their faith on Jesus Christ who died, He was buried and He rose again on the third day. They have to trust Jesus and make Him as their Lord and Savior and have that relationship with Jesus and be ready to be with Him as soon as God calls them home.

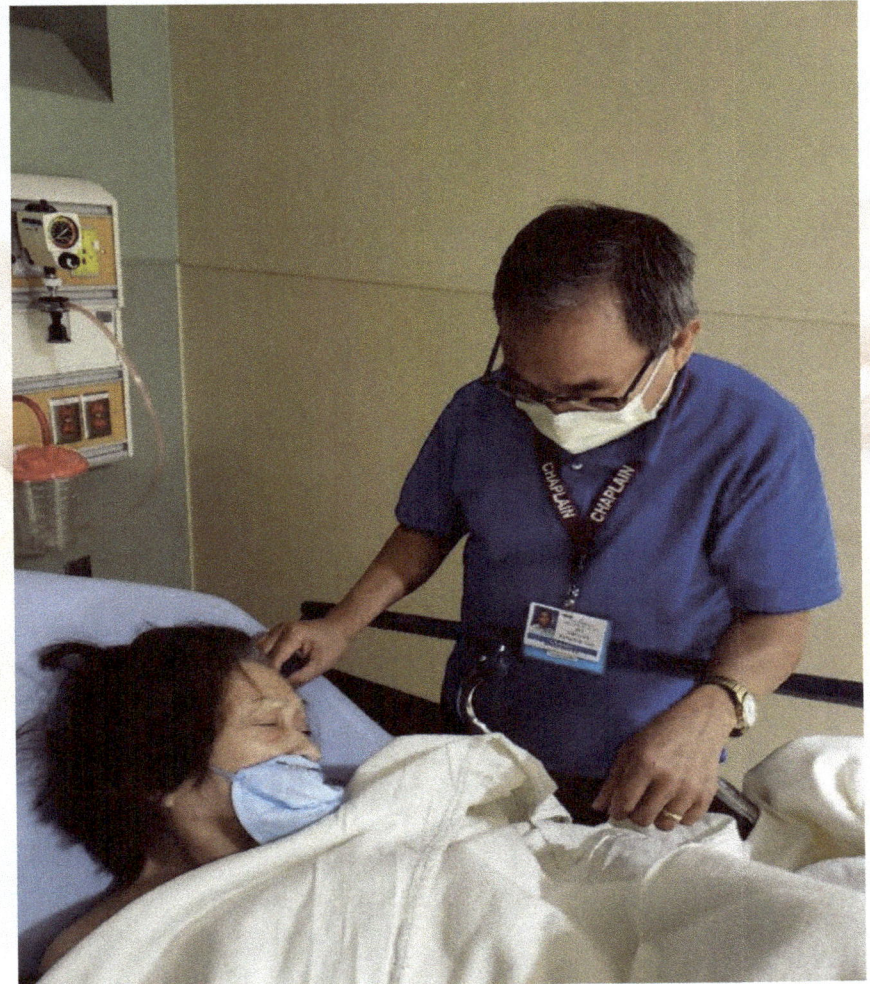

C. Parental Concern

Family members are often anxious, even to the point of being distraught, but still they hope for recovery of the patient. Thus, the usual concerns become magnified under the unfamiliar stresses; the strange sights, sounds and smell may increase the anxiety and trauma already being experience by the patient. Death anxiety, generalized apprehension, boredom, loneliness, guilt, denial of reality of their condition, irritability, depression, despair and resentment are all a part of the negativities which are experience by terminally ill patient that parents should be concern of. As Spiritual Caregiver, show your support. Often pray with them, but always ask first if they want to take the lead. Ask if there is anything that you or members of the congregation can do to assist them and their family. You may need to ask more than once. Make sure that you follow through on any promises that you make especially when you promise for a return visit to minimize the chance that family might feel abandoned by the church when they need assistance. We can offer proof of God's love for them, not only in words, but much more important is the actions.

D. Plan of Care

1. **Repentance**. As a chaplain comes to visit the patient, he must try to observe his expressions/behavior whether he is happy or not. Then try to observe his emotion and ask what makes him feel that way. Is there any thing that bothers you that you want to share? Do you have any guilty feelings that make you feel bad towards anybody? If you have done something wrong you need to settle this down. Repent and ask God to forgive you for he is always ready to forgive you from all sin.

2. **Reconciliation**. Ask the patient how are you getting along with your family. Do you have conflict with your siblings like: rivalry, jealousy, grievances, divorce in the family, or disharmony in the family? Are you willing to reconcile with them if they come and ask for forgiveness or apology for what they had done or what you have done to them. This will give you joy as you end your journey here on earth.

3. **Restoration**. On this scenario, we need to ask the family, siblings, friends to come together to restore the broken relationships and display the love for each other so that there will be peace for everyone before patient pass away.

4. **Rest**. This is the time to witness that the patient will now experience the peace of mind as well as the joy of being forgiven (**our goal**). You need to ask patient about his final wish for any sacrament offered, burial, program, sermons, preacher, hymns, person to officiate, prayers, etc.

5. **Review.** Life's review as part of this plan is to have a daily engagement of spiritual counseling, offer sacraments, prayers, Scripture reading.

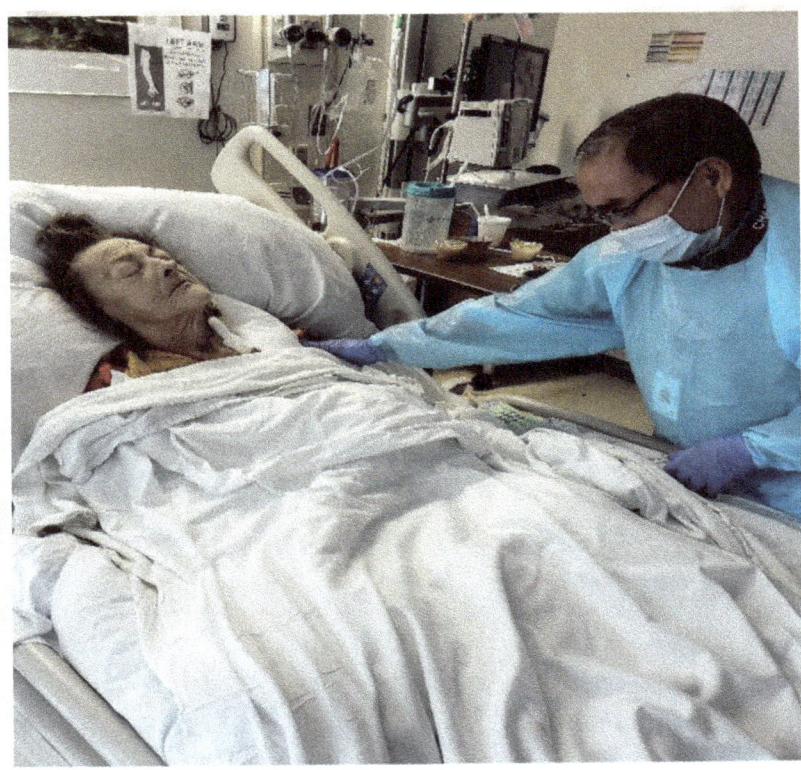

End of Life Care – A Questions to ask and, helpful Suggestions

1. What are the emotional reactions you see when you tell patients their diagnosis of terminal illness?

My experience is that the patient and family typically display the various stages of grief-denial, anger, bargaining, depression, and acceptance in addition to anxiety. These stages are not experienced in any order. Occasionally, patients and/or family remain "stuck" in one stage such as anger or depression. As a result, the stage of acceptance is never attained! The Cultural and Traditional beliefs plays a big role on this situation, that requires constant education.

2. How do you prepare family members for the final moments of their loved ones?

I feel it is important the family receive necessary education regarding the dying process and have the emotional/spiritual support they need during this difficult time. People have many different ideas about the dying process and for many it is their first experience in dealing with death. It is essential that families receive the information on what to expect so the mystery associated with death is removed and ultimately understand that death is a natural, inevitable process. I encourage questions and make every attempt to provide needed information in a way that can be understood. There are times family members do not want to discuss the dying at length and I am respectful of their wishes. Dr. Ron Naito an Internist in Portland, Ore. Who died with

Pancreatic cancer told that in order patient prepare for their death is to "Ask -Tell- Ask" about their understanding of their condition or disease and Tell straightforward and their treatment options and Ask the patient if they understood what was said so that patients can prepare their Death and their options. With that information, you can use their faith traditions and if possible get few verses in the Scripture and explain especially their personal relationship with the Lord that the patient need to be sure of their Salvation that can be found in the Lord Jesus to the end it will bring comfort, assurance and peace both the patient and family when final hours come to the dying patient to be with God in Eternity.

3. How do you cope with the stress of dealing with the terminally ill?

Palliative care team members are at high risk of developing "compassion fatigue" due to the associated stress. I find working in a multidisciplinary team with a shared goal helps me cope. Through collaboration and communication, we can be more effective which helps control stress. As a palliative care team, we also try to focus on team building activities to create a support system for one another. I have found it is also important to develop a sense of self awareness and practice self-care activities, including exercise, relation, socialization with friends/family and reading. I try to acknowledge my limitations and ask for help when I need it. I attempt to maintain a sense of balance in my life and think its important to keep one's sense of humor! Reading the book of Psalms, Proverbs, Ecclesiastes and other Scripture passages are the excellent suggestions to cope with Stress.

4. How do you handle hostility from family members?

I try to remember that the goal is not to prevent a family member from experiencing emotions such as anger, sadness, fear, and loss since these are normal responses. I feel my role is to maintain a trusting therapeutic relationship and a safe/supportive environment that allows emotions to be expressed in a positive way. I try to legitimize the appropriateness/normalcy of their reaction and try to explore what is underneath the emotion. I believe it is important to show empathy and explore strengths and strategies if possible. I often involve chaplains and social workers if the situation is very emotional. Remember the promise of God in the book of Romans chapter 12, there you, can most prepare your self the reactions of the family. The Scripture and God is what I found most helpful.

5. What are some resources you give to families?

I have a few resources I like to utilize and give to families which I have found very helpful, including the booklet, "Approaching End of Life Together: A Guide for Patients and Caregivers" by Judy Alexander, RN, CHPN and Martha J. Macri. Additional books include "A Time to Live: Living with a Life-Threatening Illness" by Barbara Karnes and "Gone from My Sight: The Dying Experience" by Barbara Karnes., Dr. H. Norman Wright " How We Can Do Serving Better the Seriously I'll and Dying ". Rev Jeffry Funk " Spiritual Needs of the Dying ".

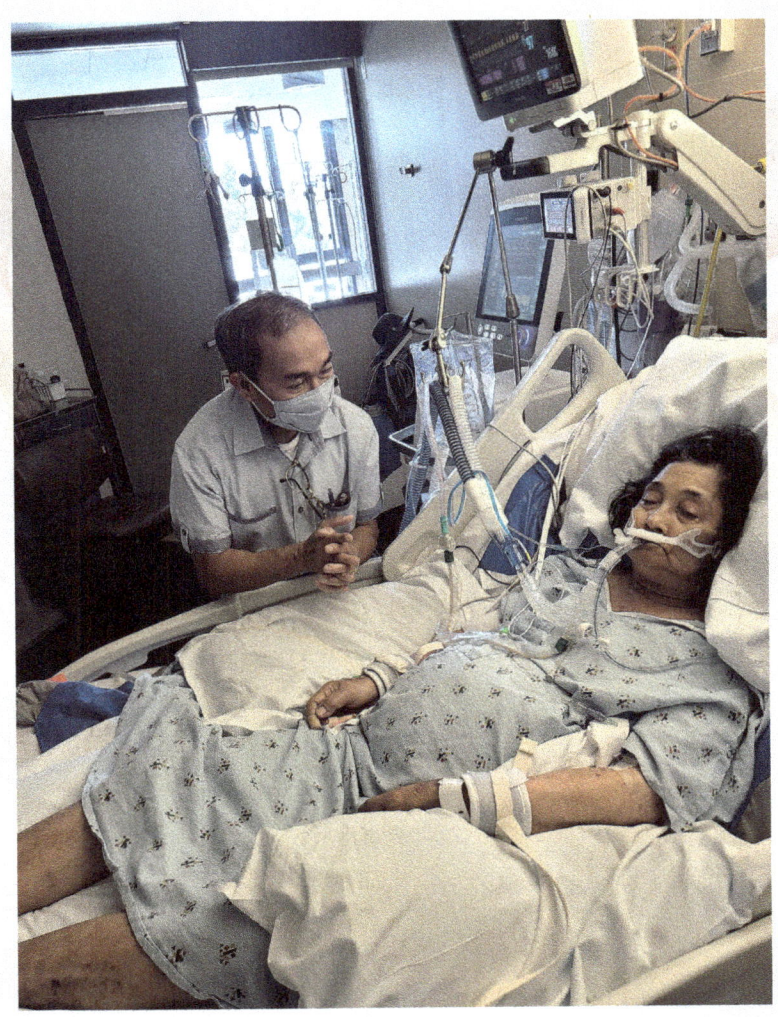

E. Penitence of Life (Life's Regrets)

Bronnie Ware says; for many years I worked in palliative care. My patients were those who had gone home to die. Some incredibly special times were shared. I was with them for the last three to twelve weeks of their lives. People grow a lot when they are faced with their own mortality. I learnt never to underestimate someone's capacity for growth. Some changes were phenomenal. Each experienced a variety of emotions, as expected, denial, fear, anger, remorse, more denial and eventually acceptance. Every single patient found their peace before they departed though, every one of them.

When questioned about any regrets they had or anything they would do differently, common themes surfaced again and again. Here are the most common regrets:

1. I wish I'd had the courage to live a life true to myself, not the life others expected of me.

This was the most common regret of all. When people realize that their life is almost over and look back clearly on it, it is easy to see how many dreams have gone unfulfilled. Most people had not honored even a half of their dreams and had to die knowing that it was due to choices they had made, or not made.

It is very important to try and honor at least some of your dreams along the way. From the moment that you lose your health, it is too late. Health brings a freedom very few realize, until they no longer have it.

2. I wish I didn't work so hard.

This came from every male patient that I nursed. They missed their children's youth and their partner's companionship. Women also spoke of this regret. But as most were from an older generation, many of the female patients had not been breadwinners. All of the men I nursed deeply regretted spending so much of their lives on the treadmill of a work existence.

By simplifying your lifestyle and making conscious choices along the way, it is possible to not need the income that you think you do. And by creating more space in your life, you become happier and more open to new opportunities, ones more suited to your new lifestyle.

3. I wish I'd had the courage to express my feelings.

Many people suppressed their feelings in order to keep peace with others. As a result, they settled for a mediocre existence and never became who they were truly capable of becoming. Many developed illnesses relating to the bitterness and resentment they carried as a result.

We cannot control the reactions of others. However, although people may initially react when you change the way you are by speaking honestly, in the end it raises the relationship to a whole new and healthier level. Either that or it releases the unhealthy relationship from your life. Either way, you win.

4. I wish I had stayed in touch with my friends.

Often they would not truly realize the full benefits of old friends until their dying weeks and it was not always possible to track them down. Many had become so caught up in their own lives that they had let golden friendships slip by over the years. There were many deep regrets about not giving friendships the time and effort that they deserved. Everyone misses their friends when they are dying.

It is common for anyone in a busy lifestyle to let friendships slip. But when you are faced with your approaching death, the physical details of life fall away. People do want to get their financial affairs in order if possible. But it is not money or status that holds the true importance for them. They want to get things in order more for the benefit of those they love. Usually though, they are too ill and weary to ever manage this task. It is all comes down to love and relationships in the end. That is all that remains in the final weeks, love and relationships.

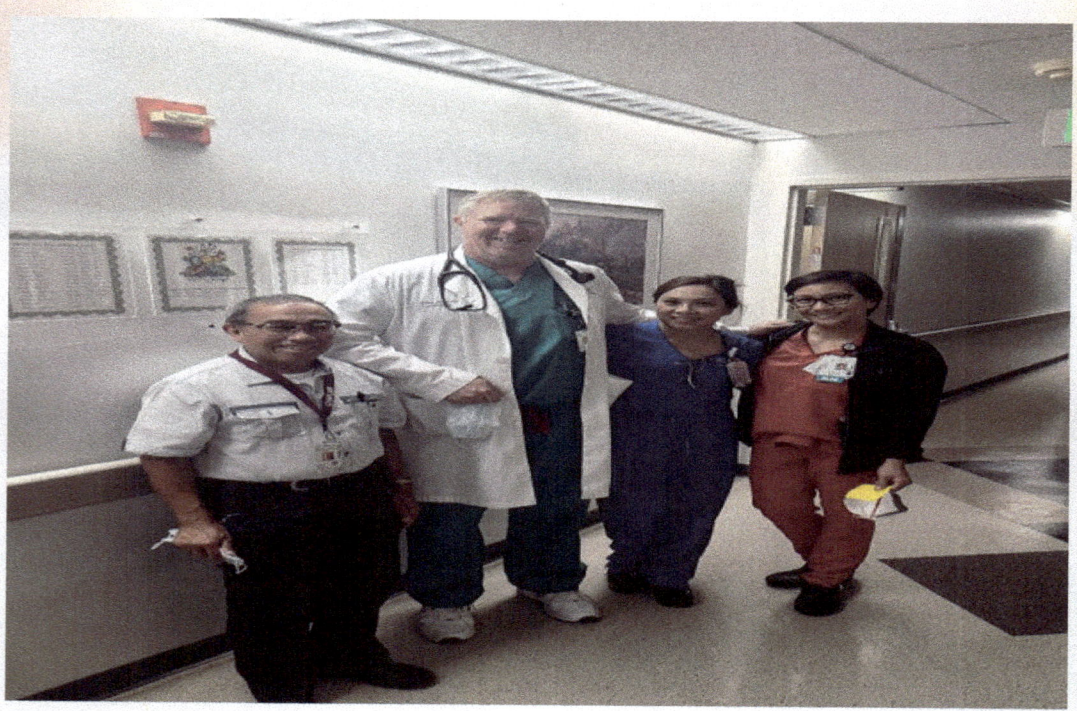

5. I wish that I had let myself be happier.

This is a surprisingly common one. Many did not realize until the end that happiness is a choice. They had stayed stuck in old patterns and habits. The so-called 'comfort' of familiarity overflowed into their emotions, as well as their physical lives. Fear of change had them pretending to others, and to their selves, that they were content. When deep within, they longed to laugh properly and have silliness in their life again. When you are on your deathbed, what others think of you is a long way from your mind. How wonderful to be able to let go and smile again, long before you are dying.

6. I wish I do what is RIGHT.

During my military years, I made many bad decisions and mistakes, that later I regret. My parents taught me both in the church and home during my early years of my Christian life to do what is Right all the time. I'm now 95 years old and hospice patient.

7. I wish I had known the Lord earlier.

During my teen age years, a good friend of mind shared the gospel and wanted me to get saved, but I refused, thinking the idea of having personal relationship with Jesus Christ is a big foolishness. I could have been die without Christ and spending the Eternal Hell, or I could ever been blessed if I open my heart to Jesus earlier, But thankful I got saved in later years of my life.

8. I wish I could serve the Lord earlier in my life.

I was taught in the Bible in Ecclesiastes 12:1 " Remember, Thy creator in thy **days of thy youth**". But I never completely obey the Lord as much as I could but fail to obey His word and has been enjoying the world instead the Lord that I don't honor the Lord's day. I could reap so many blessings that falls on me buy yet live miserably until then,

Life is a choice. It is YOUR life. Choose consciously, choose wisely, choose honestly. Choose happiness. Choose to live for God! '10 Copied 1-5, jeg 6-8

My bedside ministry has taught me a lot to the death and dying patients both in the hospital and hospice had changed my life, values, and my walk with God. jeg

44

V. Conclusion

When ministering to the terminally ill or dying patients, "be a companion to the dying person and family in a very special way." The most important skills for ministering to the dying is the capacity for compassion, which should be developed continually throughout one's ministry. A German pastor who works at a hospital gives guidance, "Words become far less important than simple gestures and a shared silence. Sitting with a family, encouraging them to hold the hand of a love one or put a cold cloth on a perspiring forehead or to moisten parched lips with water, offering prayer, brief and not prolong, or making a sign on the cross on a dying person's forehead; spelling a family member who needs to take a break or bringing coffee or soft drinks to refresh the family—each of these thoughtful gestures mean more than a thousand words. At the time of death, supporting them in touching the body and talking to it, protecting their privacy as each close relative may want to say good-bye separately and which might help them cry and crying with them, if the tears are there, will speak profoundly of the pastor's care for them and of the Lord's compassionate love"8.

Families may appreciate joining hands around the bed of the deceased, along with nurses and friends, for prayer of thanksgiving for person's life and commendation of the person's keeping. Words of comfort for the family should be included and a brief Scripture passage. The pastor should take seriously the dying person's premonitions about his death. They may have dreams in which the deceased parents call the dying person to join them. The pastor may help the dying person by encouraging him to tell his life story. Many people can sum up their lives in a few stories from their past. In listening, the pastor can help the dying person find peace, wholeness, completion of life, and acceptance of death.

Be supportive to the family and friends as they grieve and release the dying. Grief causes pain, and the bereaved need understanding, patience, and acceptance. No matter how long a person may anticipate death of a love one, the actual moment is still painful experience, though there may be also a deep sense of relief-both for self and for the person who died.

During this time of crisis, you can assess and understand their self-image and discover how it affects them. As a Spiritual caregiver, you can keep an open communication with the ones left behind. Help them to see a light at the end of the tunnel they are passing through and there is hope. You are the helper God has called to walk with them through this transition of crisis. Your prayer and support makes a difference in the life of the dying person. Remember, be Compassionate, Loving, Sacrifice and be Prayerful that resonate your life as Spiritual Caregiver. Mark 1:41 " Jesus, moved with Compassion". Matthew 9:35 " Jesus went about all cities,.. healing all manner of diseases."

May God richly bless you in this worth rewarding ministry you are engage!

Bibliography

1.   Allen Tong, MD. General Medicine, UC Davis Medical Center, Sacramento, CA

2.   Crisis and Trauma Counseling; Dr. Norman Wright; Regal Books; 2003

3.   Janice Noort, NP, Palliative Dept. UC Davis Medical Center, Sacramento, CA

4.   John McMillan, MD, Medical Director, UC Davis Hospice, Sacramento, CA

5.   Love Your Patients ; Scott Louis Diering; Blue Dolphin Publishing; 2004

6.   Making Sense Out of Suffering; Peter Kreeft; St Anthony Messenger Press;1986

7.   Ministering to the Ill and Dying Children and their Families; Pat Fosarelli; Liguori Publication; 2003

8.   The Mourning Handbook; Helen Fitzgerald; The Fireside Book; 1994

9.   The Hospital Handbook; Lawrence D. Reimer & James T. Wagner; Morehouse Publishing;1984

10.   Bonnie Ware – RN, 'The Top Five Regrets of the Dying – A Life Transformed by the Dearly Departing'.